The Valley of Your Life

ekphrastic poems

Mari-Carmen Marin

The Valley of Your Life

ekphrastic poems

SHANTI ARTS PUBLISHING
BRUNSWICK, MAINE

The Valley of Your Life

Published by Shanti Arts Publishing

Designed by Shanti Arts Designs

Shanti Arts LLC
193 Hillside Road
Brunswick, Maine 04011

shantiarts.com

Cover image is *Serenity*, by the Mallorcan painter
Tomás Ortega Díaz. Available on Wikimedia Commons.

Printed in the United States of America

ISBN: 978-1-962082-24-2 (softcover)

Library of Congress Control Number: 2024935914

Papá, tu cariño, apoyo, y fé en quien soy y lo que soy capaz de hacer me motivan cada día a buscar la luz que a veces se esconde tras las partes más oscuras de mi vida. Este libro va dedicado a ti.

CONTENTS

ACKNOWLEDGMENTS

The author extends her heartfelt thanks to Tupelo Press for its Zoom Online Manuscript Conference in January 2023 and to Jeffrey Levine's careful editing of the full manuscript of this collection. Their expertise, guidance, and love for poetry have left an indelible mark.

The author wishes to thank the editors of the following publications in which these poems, some in earlier forms, previously appeared:

Discretionary Love Magazine: "Stood Up," April 10, 2022.

The Ekphrastic Review: "The Colors of My Past, Present, and Future," Horace Pippin Ekphrastic Writing Challenge, June 5. 2020; "Spinning Yarn," July 5, 2020; "The Thief," August 10, 2022.

Emerge Literary Journal: "Condemned to Live," 2023.

The Magnolia Review: "Solitude," March 16, 2023

Months to Years: "Abuela, What Will I Do without You?" Winter 2021.

Pandemic Poems (Virus Anthology): "Abuela, What Will I Do without You?" Finalist, Public Poetry, July 2022.

Poetica Review: "Consumed by Pain" and "My Mirror," Autumn 2020.

The Poetic Bond X, edited by Trevor Maynard, Willowdown Books: "The Old Guitarist" (appears here as "Pablo's Blues"), Fall 2020.

Poets' Choice: Corona Global Lockdown, edited by Akshay Sonthalia: "A Screaming Man in a Lonely World" (appears here as "Oh! A Lonely Man in a Lonely World"), July 7, 2020.

Spillwords Press: "El Día de los Muertos," November 1, 2020.

Speckled Trout Review: "Vincent's Night Sky," Spring 2021.

Wordriver Literary Review: "The Joys of Contemplation," Spring 2009.

ON THE OTHER SIDE

—Tomás Ortega Díaz, *Serenidad*, Spain, 2018 (cover image)

"The best way out is always through."
—Robert Frost

When life spirals out of control,
despair sucks you into its empty center
like a vortex around your neck, shoulder
blades, waist, legs, feet. You resist, grab
the first object at hand—a tree branch,
a steel rod, a barbed-wire fence. Your fingers
get raw, weak, sweaty, slippery. You see
yourself vacuumed, dislodged, dismembered, a speck
of dust in the cosmos. You freeze your pain
till its numbness awakens your tears.

What if you stand facing your tornado?
Join the force, the light, the energy
around you. Take off your shoes.
Mark your footprints on the first
step you take. Climb the ladder
between your turbulence
and the quietude on the other side.
Jump.

Painters have often taught writers how to see.

—James Baldwin

THE DANCE OF LIFE

—Salvador Dali, *Ravel's Bolero (Le Boléro)*, 1946

When your life becomes a desert—sand shifting, burying your path,
dance.

When your fertile past is a mirage—the sun blinding you till you become the night,
dance.

When the sky can't be your anchor—changing from yellow to petrol to emerald at dusk,
dance.

Wear your gilet, your toreador pants, your bright red tops, capes, and turbans.
Swirl your golden, white, and blue skirts in the wind.
Let the ribbons around your wrists, your waist, your knees, your neck, your hands, move with the rest
of your body.

Climb up a stone arch.
Put on your hat.
Play a bolero with your Spanish guitar, and if you can't,
sit close to the dancers and players.

Mountains of turquoise and purple will pop up, blend with the dancers' colors, and you will dance
from your desert   to   the valley of your
life.

I

FOUNTAINS, GARDENS, AND THE HUNGER FOR MORE

THE WRITER, THE ENCHANTER

—Remedios Varo, *The Juggler (The Magician)*, 1956

I like to touch
the hearts of the crowds, hold

their eyes, awed at my juggling
of words,

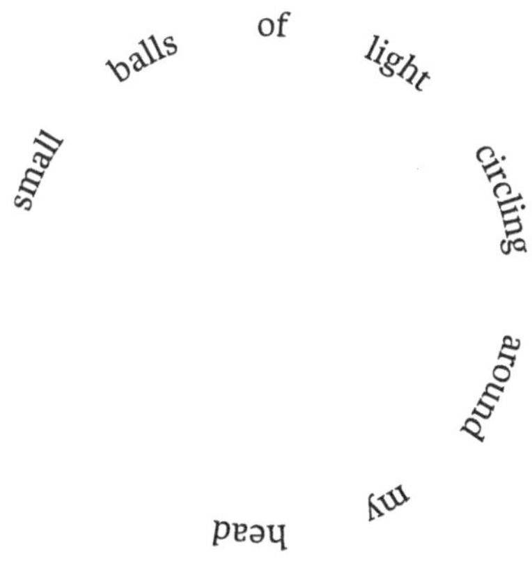

like some stardust. I practice
my magic for those who walk by daylight

but are asleep. Robed
in the same cloak, they share

the need to wake, to see
that life is more

than an office, a desk and a laptop, bank notes,
ibuprofen, valium, clearance items, BMWs, diets, feasts, an orgasm.

I give them a gleam of my light in hope they realize
that their experiences, their feelings are unlike

mine, unlike others', that we all
can be writers of our lives.

MY FANTASY GARDEN

—Joan Miró, *The Garden*, 1925

My garden must be as colorful as Miró's,

                    that pale blue of a cloudless sky

that kisses the sloppy ground of perfect green, red grass
that never dies, the canvas for each living creature,

                              with its concentric flowers,

each circle a color of orange, dark or light green,
yellow, red, blue, or black,   flowers
that never trigger itchy eyes, runny noses, or a marathon of sneezes,

                                        with lingering floral scents,

                    without insects that sting and bite and turn

the skin of my legs and arms into a land of little volcanoes erupting
with pus and angry red,

                    with harmless unnamed critters: the snake-

like caterpillar with pink face and black wavy body,

the half-chicken-half-dove bird

with rosy chest,
the exceedingly tall ant with checkered

abdomen and black thorax as if wearing a winged silk shawl,

the peacock-and-ostrich as one, shaped

like two quavers—a musical touch,

the funnel-faced parrot reaching for the star

of the garden,

and feelers, lots of feelers,

so much needed to connect
with others and remind us not to step
out-of-bounds.

ETERNAL DESIRE

—Gustav Klimt, *The Kiss,* 1907 or 1908

Take me to that place where time
stands still and sunlight scatters
across the sky through cosmic dust
while we are bathed   i n
                                                  g o l d e n
                                                  r a i n.

Lock me in your manly embrace,
then throw the key into the abyss below
my feet.

Ground me in the patch
of wildflowers, grassy as we kneel, wrapped
in a bubble of eternity.

Kiss me until your lips
have covered my body, north
                                        to
                                        south,
west   to   east.

Let your vertical
                                        rec
                                        t   an
                                        gles

merge with

my
les   ci
rc

in an

e x p

l o s

i o n

o f

g o

l d

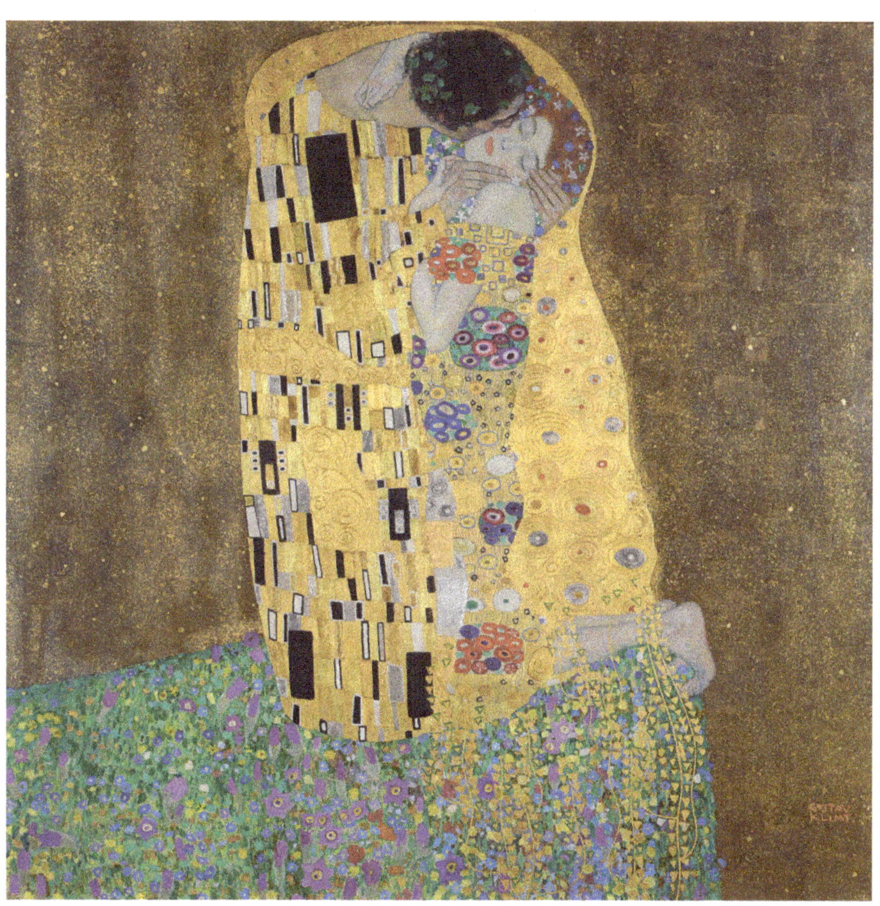

Gustav Klimt, *The Kiss*

CHAMELEONING MY WAY TO YOU

—James Bullough, *Linger*, 2020

If granted a superpower, I would blend into the grey

leather of your car seats, the brown nylon of your studio

carpet, the stainless steel door of your refrigerator,

your bedroom's wallpaper, blue

with red nine-petal flowers,

so that I could know

the ground your feet trod,

your new work projects, your

latest cravings. I wonder if you still dread

Sundays, if your drawing hands silence

the voice of your anger, if you sleep naked, your body heat

stirring my embers, the taste of your skin lingering beneath my tongue.

SPINNING YARN

—Remedios Varo, *Dead Leaves (Les Feuilles Mortes)*, 1956

My fountain is dry, lost in the confines
of the empty hallways of *mis entrañas.*
Death surrounds me: an old carpet, fading
like the green in a dead patch of grass.
Ceiling, walls, mantelpiece, chairs, all
are covered in dying moss.

Help me find my water, *mi musa amada.*
Pull some life from me with your magic thread,
the singing birds *de la luz, del amor, de la paz.*
Guide them through to the outside
world, the breeze brushing the curtains apart.
Let them see your earthy skin touched
only by the green of your spring-leaf gown, your
waist-long hair, lit by the fire of Apollo. Show me
the way back to the garden of unending words.

FEELING ALIVE

—Michelle Constantine, *Dance of Passion*, 2012

What is life without the storm,
the dark veil covering
the blue sky, like smoke
eating up the oxygen
in a room on fire,
the bolt of lightning followed
by the scream of thunder?

What is life without the geyser
bursting energy into the air
burning the soil
around my feet
and the feet that dare
to come after me?

What is life without the wording and the words,
the flesh and bones
of thoughts roaring in my head,
then, uttered,
shooting
blood up
and down the body?

What is life without the dance and the dancer
propelled by the heat
of one body against another,
the love and the lover
two people,
one heart
pumping at once,
the clap that keeps me tapping
and the clapper?

II

THE NOW IS A GIFT, THAT IS WHY THEY CALL IT THE PRESENT

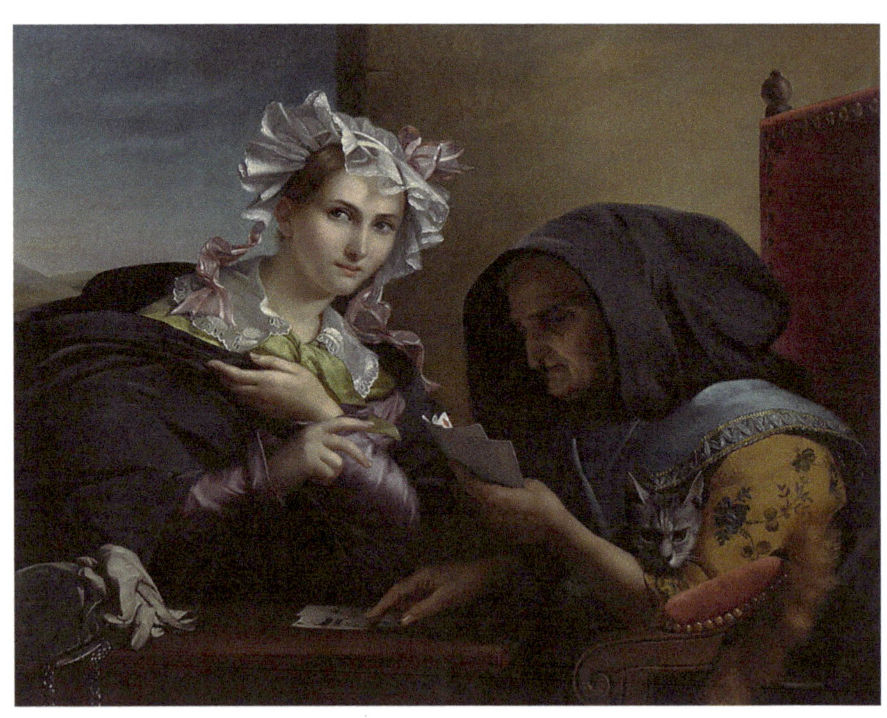

Adele Kindt, *The Fortune Teller*

THE THIEF

—Adele Kindt, *The Fortune Teller*, 1835

The future holds treasures she wants to uncover
as eagerly as she removes her hooded cloak
from over her shoulders, her unblemished skin

a soft-hued marble slab in a museum. Youth
makes her heart thirsty, a thirst only a fortune
teller may quench with the help of cards. With lines

harrowing her coarsened face, the old swindler seems
to hold the key to the mystery of what is not but it will
be. She hides behind her black hood and holds on tight

to her black cat, as if darkness could help light
come alive. Outside, the blue sky wears pink ribbons,
its nightgown's flirty frills. *Don't you see?*

It screams for all to hear. *The future you hope to discover*
stands here, in front of you. Anything else is a thief.

LIFE'S LITTLE PLEASURES

—Kadir Nelson, *Heat Wave*, 2019

When the summer heat bakes the streets
of Brooklyn, I stay indoors, always in front
of the fan. Its humming keeps me company,
my daily August soundtrack, until the sun
dismisses the day and admits the night.

With the curtains pulled back, as in a theater, I am
the star of my neighborhood. I lean out of my brownstone
window, wearing my dreadlocks in an updo. With half
a glass of water to resuscitate my wilting plant in one hand,
I close my eyes, breathe in the evening and pretend
not to see my naughty puggle steal a few licks of the fresh
layer popsicle I hold in my other hand.

THE JOYS OF CONTEMPLATION

—Salvador Dali, *Girl at the Window*, 1925

She has a secret,
a hiding place
where time disappears,
a room of free space,
a benefit of the austere.

The ecru wall
opens itself to a stunning view,
a miracle of light, a breath of air
that entrances her,
draws her away from earthly despair.

The sky and the sea
each reflects the other's placidness,
a performance
of harmony, sound, and motion:
the water dancing

to the rhythm of the attuned waves,
to the melody of the lulling breeze,
inviting an enthusiastic sailboat
to follow her steps
and enjoy her ease.

—*continued*

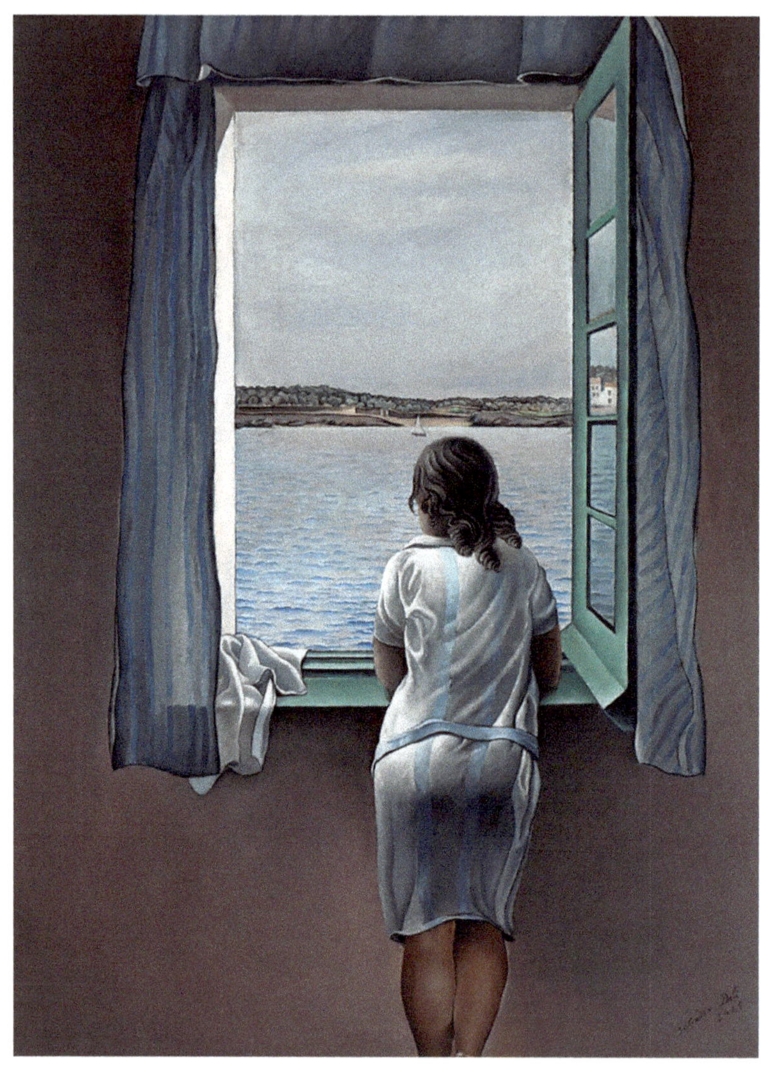

Salvador Dali, *Girl at the Window*

The wide mouth of the Cadaqués bay
opens to a small town,
as if to warm her cool immensity
with cordial greens and calid browns.

A few white houses
with tawny roofs
blend with the landscape
of gray slate and olive grooves.

Lost in contemplation,
she is part of creation,
light as the air that swells her lungs
with a saline current of renewed life.

Her warm skin
shares the tan of the earth.
Dim gray spiral shells
cover her head,
floating on the curvy bright sea of her clothes,
dancing with the waves of their indigo blue stripes
and the jaunty drapes.

The earth, the sky, the sea become her,
merged with nature.
bathed in bliss.

THE COLORS OF MY ROOM

—Vincent van Gogh, *The Bedroom*, 1889

Walls: pale as the lavender fields of Provence.
Floor: copper red; its brightness recedes like a tide.
Bed, chairs, and picture frames wood: ocher, like the sunflowers in the south of France.
Sheets and pillows: ashy yellow, like the early morning sunlight.
Coverlet: as a sunset sky.
Window blinds: green, as a grassland.
Toilet table: orange, like chrysanthemums.
Basin: Mediterranean blue.
Doors: like trees of purple lilac.

With nature tones
I turn my bedroom
into a place of repose.

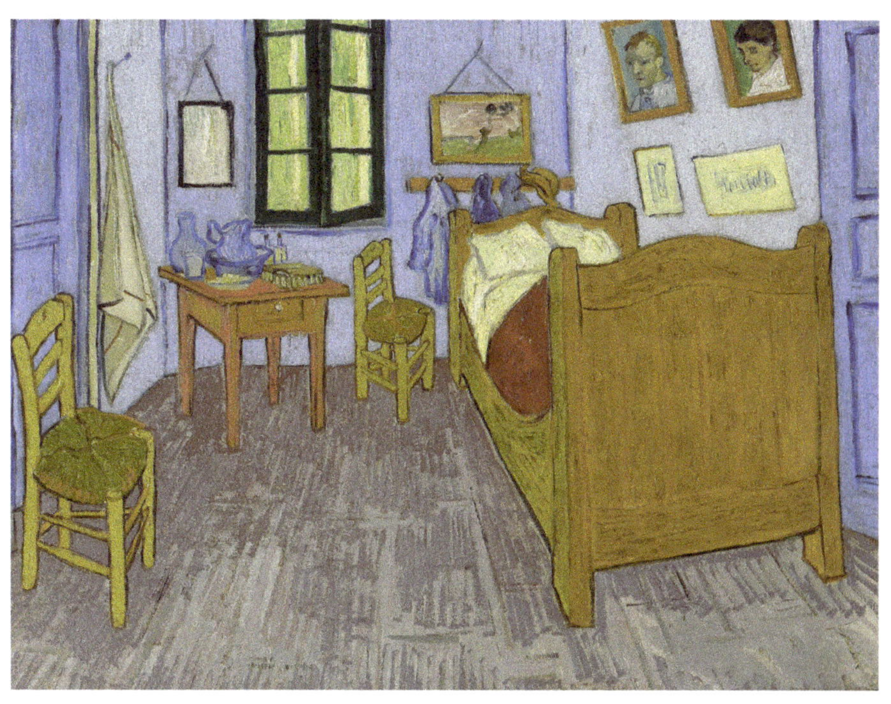

Vincent van Gogh, *The Bedroom*

III

CAMINANTE, NO HAY CAMINO,
SE HACE CAMINO AL ANDAR

—Antonio Machado

NIGHTMARES OF HISTORY

—Zdzislaw Beksinski, *Untitled*, second half of twentieth century

Clouds of smoke and dirt. The city suffocates. German bombings.

Buildings gutted by fires and more fires.

In the hellish day, the monster,

blue cavities for eyes

mouth as mammoth as

a giant's cave,

sucks in ← Polish
victims as a vast vacuum cleaner would swallow ← all debris from a
demolition site.
An army of humanoid spiders, crawling
or dead and carried on top of stormtroopers'
backs, march to their end: death
by hatred.

BERGEN-BELSEN CONCENTRATION CAMP, APRIL 1945

—Doris Clare Zinkeisen, *The Human Laundry: Belsen, April 1945*

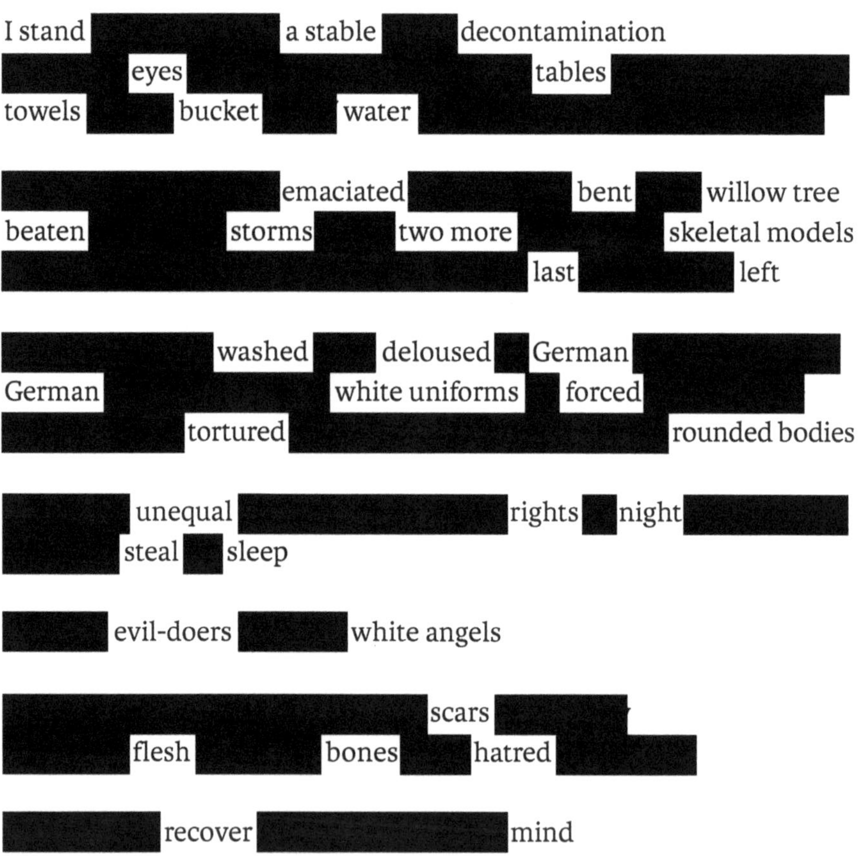

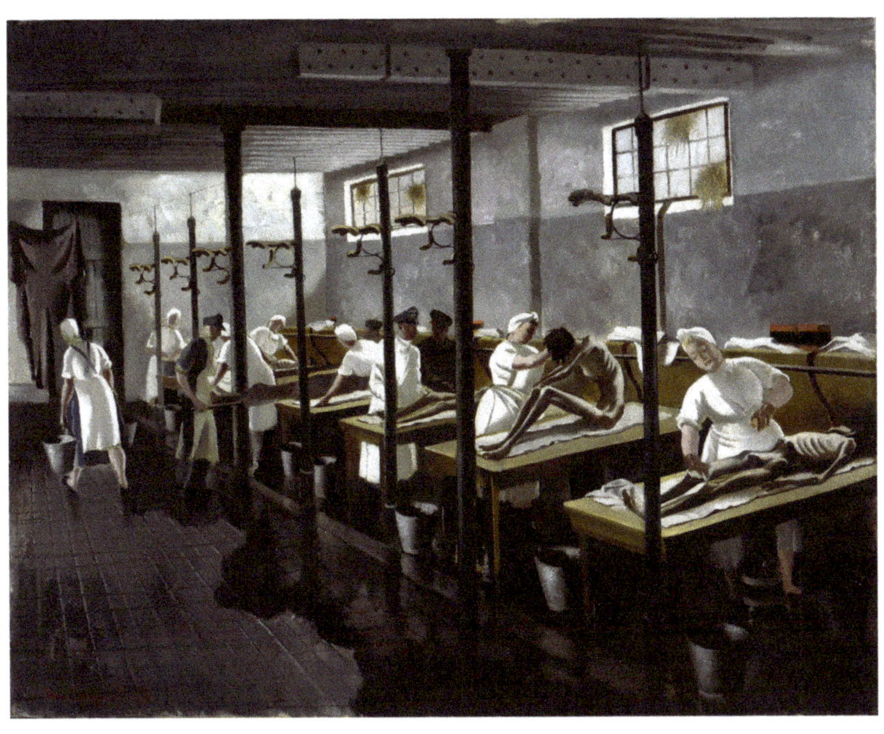

Doris Clare Zinkeisen, *The Human Laundry: Belsen, April 1945*

BITTER REVENGE—A TRAGEDY—ACT 3 SCENE 1

—Francesco Hayez, *Vengeance is Sworn*, 1851

RACHEL Let's wreak vengeance on the one you thought faithful, him
who swore he'd rather poke his eyes out than look at another

woman. Doesn't he deserve to burn with the flames
of your rage? Shouldn't he have a taste of your shame?

(Rachel has proof of his new love and his betrayal, all in one letter, no reference made to months of flirting that she's hidden behind her mask of deception. Who is the friend? Who's the traitor? Mary knows well, but she resists the urge to hurt who hurt her first. Her blindfold off)

MARY what for?

Can the blood seeping
through his wounds stop my own,

can his tears wash away the bruises
staining my amour propre,

can the pain narrowing his eyes
help unfurrow my brow,

will I arise, an embittered
phoenix, from his ashes,

or will the sugar of revenge
cloy my appetite for love?"

(She pushes Rachel off, lest she have second thoughts on avenging not one but two wrongs).

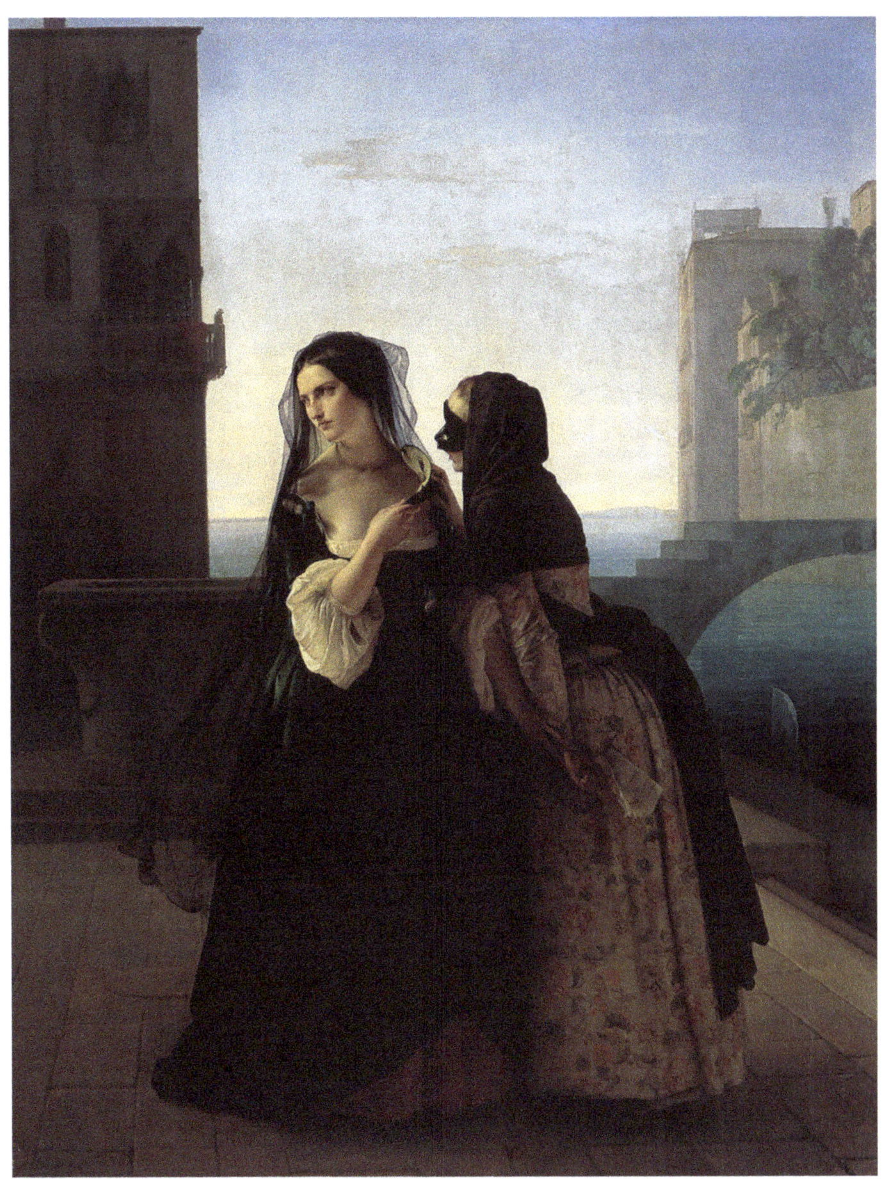

Francesco Hayez, *Vengeance is Sworn*

THE BOAT AND THE BEACON

—Leonid Afremov, *Boat by the Lighthouse*

A solitary sailboat rested at anchor,
cradled by the motionless harbor sea.
Its surface mirrored the sunset sky,
rich hues of red blending with orange,
crimson and purple.

As the sailboat swayed to a lullaby
of waves, the surrounding waters
were bathed in a pool of brightness
emanating from a tall beacon, whose
light kept the boat company all night.

Once the beacon's vigil ended at sunrise—
a brisk breeze blowing—the boat's owner
embarked and set sail to the next harbor,
leaving the beacon behind.

IV

IT ALL BEGINS AND ENDS WITH LOVE

THE VEIL THAT BURNED

—Rene Magritte, *The Lovers II,* 1928

Dan began to come to class earlier each day.
Mar moved her lessons to the balcony of her apartment.
Dan loved the sights of the palm trees, and the beach across the street.
Mar saw he was lonely and joined him for walks after classes.

Dan enjoyed the salty breeze and the smells from the bars along
the beach walk.
Mar took him for tapas in a chiringuito called Tio Pepe.
Dan couldn't have enough of calamares en salsa.
Mar loved seeing him smile.
Dan didn't want to go home those nights.
Mar didn't want these days to end.
Mar was twenty-seven
Dan was twenty-nine.
Mar knew he was not available—men like him were hard to find.
Dan knew his girlfriend waited for him to be with her in one month.

And yet, they spent most of their time together, speaking Spanish
during class, English after each lesson, and the common language
coming from the heart during the silences in between their words,
in the narrow space between their bodies, where her lips were dying
to bite his lips, and his tongue was yearning to touch her tongue,
a veil of restraint covering their heads, trying to stop the unstoppable
desire to possess and be possessed, to merge her flames with
his flames and become one big fire.

Lying on the beach at sunset towards the end of the
summer, their bodies almost touching, he looked
into her eyes, burning the veil around them to ashes.

MY MIRROR

—Remedios Varo, *The Lovers*, 1963

A storm is blowing up inside you. Gusty
winds roar through your ears, while
monsoon rains flood in between your
bones and boiling blood, after lightning
bolts have burnt your spirit. Staying still,
you are paralyzed by the shock.
I'm sitting beside you in the park,
hand-in-hand. Now, your winds, your rains,
your lightning strikes are also mine. From
your chest through my chest, then out,
a grey cloud departs our bodies, flies up
towards sullen skies, escorted by two tall
evergreens that ground us among the chaos.
Through you, I see
my world; you breathe my air.
I speak your words. Murky
waters may rise, but you'll never drown.
I am with you, riding out your storms.

STOOD UP

—Amrita Sher-Gil, *Sumair*, 1936

I put on my grandmother's silk saree. She
wore it just once, on her sister's wedding
day, then passed it on to my mother, who
passed it on to me when I turned thirteen.

I clip on my emerald earrings and apply
rouge to my cheeks and lips. The finishing
touch: I have stuck two petunias into my
neatly coifed bun. Enveloped in the green

of pasture fields—pink brush strokes forming
petals that float on the ripples of the fabric
of my garment—I wait for you on a bench
in The Hanging Gardens. But you never arrive.

I have become the flowers in my hair, now
in my hand—droopy, ready to be dumped
and left behind. Gathering around, thick
clouds of green obliterate the sun.

OH! A LONELY MAN IN A LONELY WORLD

—Edvart Munch, *The Scream*, 1893

A man on a winter bridge in Oslo, 1893,
senses a disturbance in nature: blood-red flames
seem to burn the sky in horizontal waves. A maelstrom
in a blue-black fjord sucks in the fire above, while the hill
to its right side struggles to contain the water's turmoil.
The man stops in panic; his two friends continue
their walk oblivious. His skull-like face starts to deform
in terror. His hands, elongated, cover his ears
to protect him from nature's shriek of pain,
felt through his body, twisting, squirming.

Year 2020. I want to scream like the man on the bridge in Oslo.
I'm vanishing, blending into my home walls, living a life of
non-living, each day a clone of the others, all human touch
forbidden. When in public, masks cover mouths
and noses, gloves protect hands, eyes avoid looking
at other eyes—no room for connection—we stand
six feet apart, separated by tall screens. The fear
of dying is stronger than our need for warmth. A greedy
virus threatens to suck all air from our lungs, like the maelstrom
in the blue-black fjord sucking the fire in from the flaming sky above.

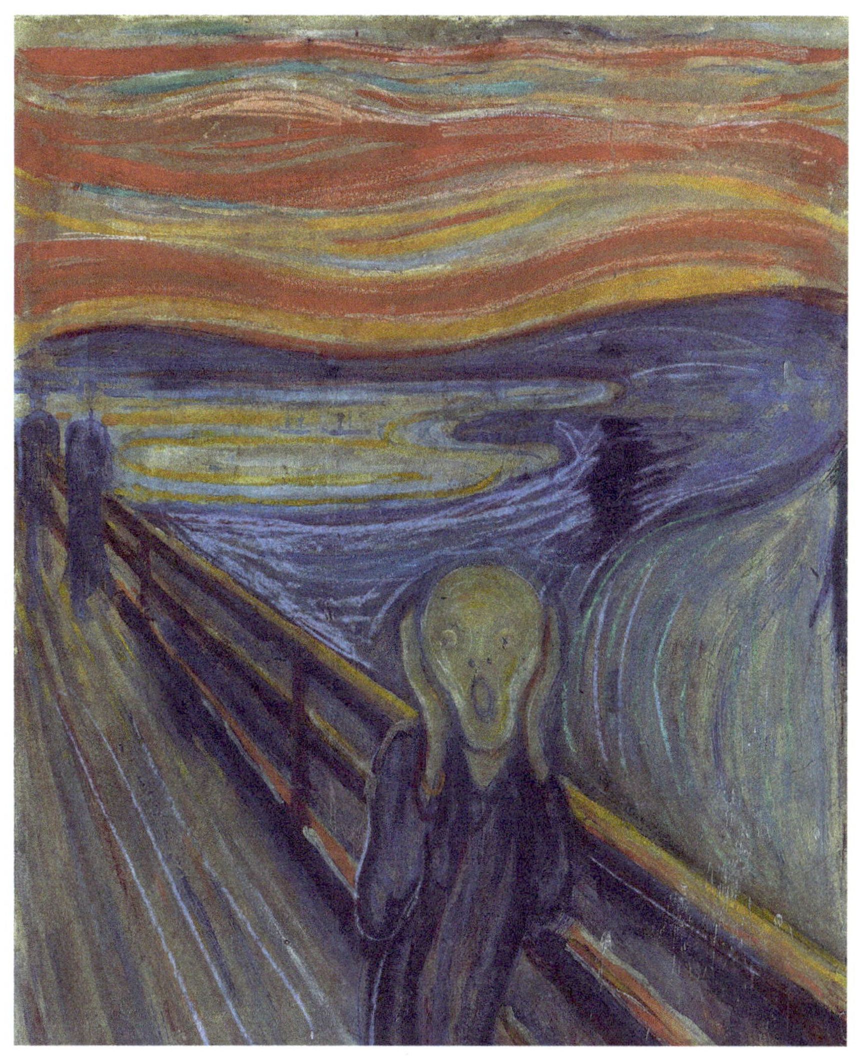

Edvart Munch, *The Scream*

ABUELA, WHAT WILL I DO WITHOUT YOU?

—by Juan Lucena *¿Qué Haremos sin Ellos? (What Will We Do without Them?)*, 2020

You drove two hundred
miles to welcome me into the world.
Despite my puffy face and wrinkly skin,
you called me the most precious baby.
You cradled me to sleep.

When I could not stop crying—too much light,
too much noise, too cold, too hot, too small
to know what was wrong—you lifted me so I
rested my head on your shoulder, my tummy
pressing against your body, you sang "Hush,
Little Baby" until your soothing voice lulled
my fright and I felt safe upon your chest.

I took my first steps into your outstretched arms
and licked my first taste of cake from your fingers
when I turned one. You loved to sit me on your lap
and read "You and Me, Little Bear," every time
that I said "Again."

You let me sit on a kitchen highchair next to you while you cooked *paella* and I asked you if I could help; you gave me cut pieces of grapes and bananas when the smell of the *sofrito* made me hungry. You stayed with me when I was sick and could not go to school. If I was scared, you sat at the end of my bed until I went to sleep.

Three months ago, you were taken to the hospital with a virus called Corona, but there was no crown, no throne, nor subjects to visit you there. I wanted to grab your wrinkled hands and put cream and a bandage wherever it hurt, like the time you hit your leg on the leg of your bed and your skin scraped off. I wanted to show you the new books I had read since school closed and we must stay at home. But I could not see you through the tall screen of fear that separated you from me.

Now that *mami* has said you are gone forever
I just want to know, what will I do without you?

V

BRING IT ON

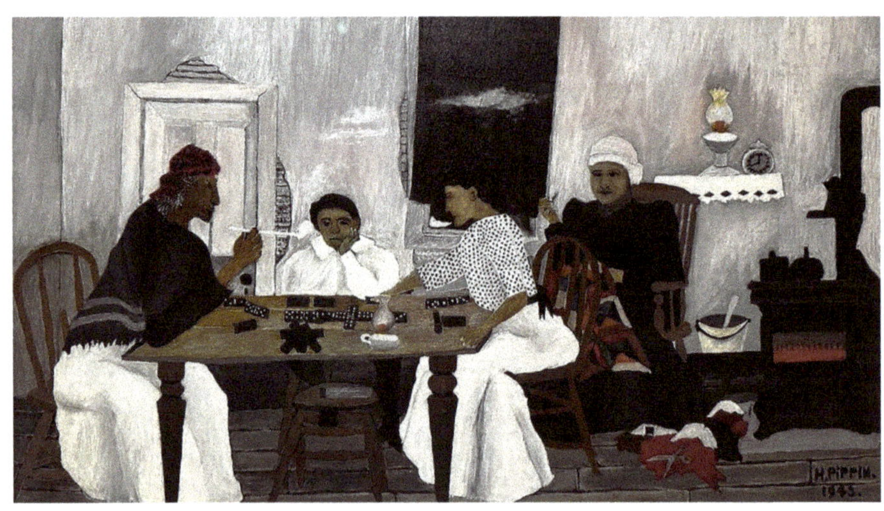

Horrace Pippin, *Domino Players*

THE COLORS OF MY PAST, PRESENT, AND FUTURE

—Horace Pippin, *Domino Players*, 1943

Sunday evenings we played dominoes for hours on the kitchen
table: the black tiles with white pips inverted the pattern of mom's
black polka-dot blouse, her and grandma's white skirts tuned up
to my aunt's black poncho top and white head scarf, my white shirt
combined with black pants and shoes, a white doily was crossed

with black diamond shapes on our only shelf, and a white bucket
sat next to a black coal-burning stove. Another color, the red
of the blood shed by my people, enslaved and exploited like
grandma, lay on the floor on a red scrap of cloth that my aunt
used for quilting, while grandma, letting white smoke waft out

from her white pipe, wore the red on her head scarf as a badge
of honor. The also red warmth from the coal fire and the flames
from the oil lamps would always light my way as a black person
living in a white world. Out of the window, a grey cloud floated
freely in the dark sky of Goshen, New York.

WORDS TO MY SON ON HIS TWELFTH BIRTHDAY

—Neena Sethia, *Contradictions of Being*, 2021

I cannot help but admire your journey from a boy to a man:

Your white skin, your blonde wavy hair,
your long neck, your masculine nose
as if sculpted by the hands of Phidias.
You look at others with curious eyes, seek
their approval, acceptance, a sense of belonging
you find when wearing your merging cloak,
that teal blanket that helps you keep warm and safe
but that you can throw any time you need
to be you, the only light shining in the ocean
on a starless night.

But I must tell you something about this world:

There are some without cloaks
to wear or remove at will, their skin
darker than yours; their bodies
become objects to use, abuse,

and discard. Stared at but never
seen. Shackled in groups they
cannot leave. Their necks
will be cut if they speak their voices.
They must carry whiteness on their heads
like racing horses wear blinders
on either side of their eyes.

Know that you have power to change what you do not like:

Be the white dove with the plucked leaf
in your mouth, help others grow wings
on their heads to fly free. Like the shadow
under dead leaves, our spirit can never
be shackled or killed.

ONION TEARS

—Lilly Martin Spencer, *Peeling Onions*, 1852

She merges into the wooden counter
in her kitchen, "a woman's place,"
until she disappears.

A worker of miracles, each day she
turns poultry, fruits, and vegetables touched
by signs of decay into a life-giving meal for her

husband and four children. No days off, no
salary, no raise. She is not allowed mistakes.
She has no help. She is a server, never

served. She should not complain—her worth
is at stake. Yet I see her beyond the shadows.
The half-cut onion in her firm grip could have

never caused her red swollen eye, the tears she tries
to hold in place, her downturned brow and lips. She needs
a friend to enter her private space. She must realize she can

hold the knife in the hand that wipes tears from her face.
She knows how to keep its sharp edge away.
She has strong arms.

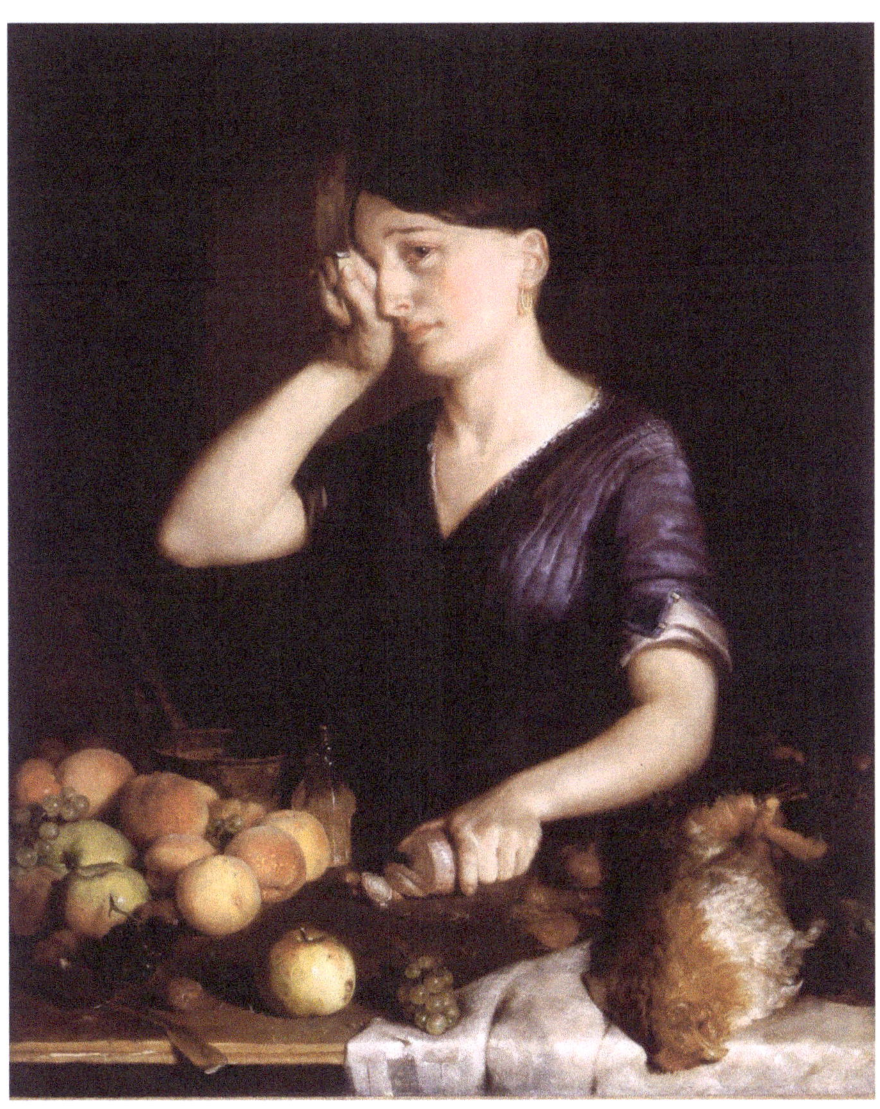

Lilly Martin Spencer, *Peeling Onions*

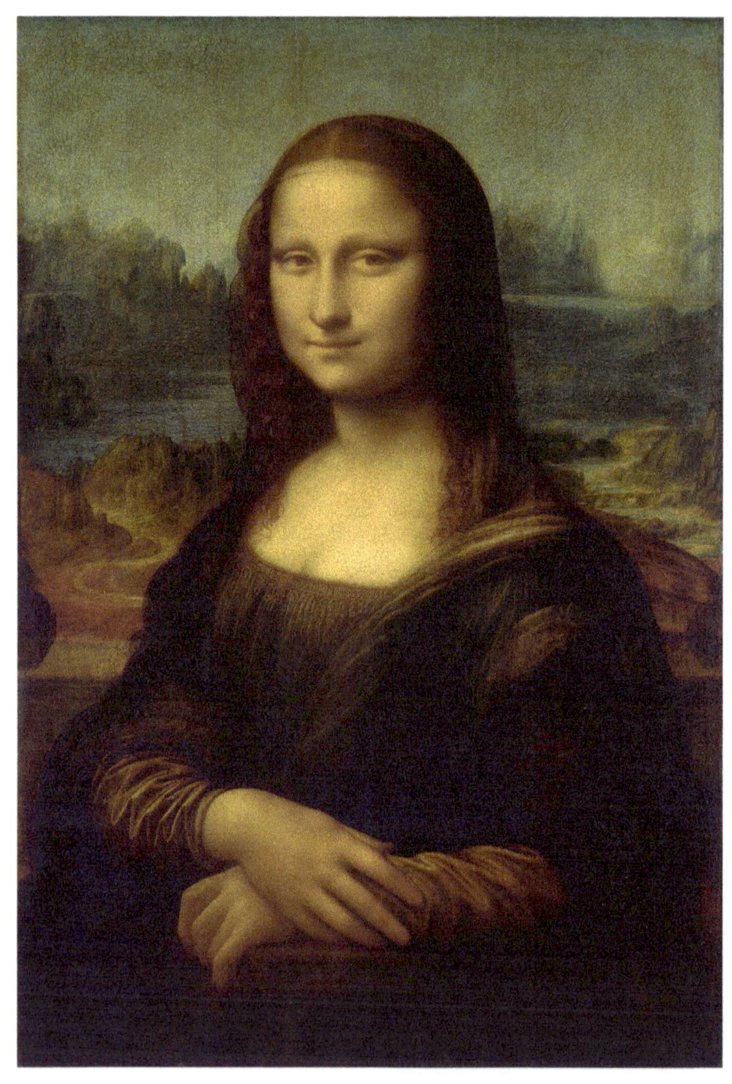

Leonardo da Vinci, *Mona Lisa*

I SEE THE PAIN IN YOUR SMILE

—Leonardo da Vinci, *Mona Lisa,* 1503–19

Happy, fancy clothes in the sixteenth-century
Florentine fashion, in an open loggia with dark
pillar bases on each side, behind you a vast
landscape of rivers, mountains, and valley.

How long you sat for da Vinci with your delicate
veil, your finely wrought tresses, your soft-
sculptured face, every fold of fabric, your curves.

Now you have your own room in the Louvre, natural
light from a glass ceiling, and constant flood of love
letters, flowers, a little spotlight to enhance your colors.

And yet, there is something faint and aloof in the air,
like a firefly caught in a glass vase. The winding road,
the bridge, the wild rocks and water stretching

to the horizon behind you are fake, a promise
denied to women meant to marry young, produce
children, stay indoors, like porcelain dolls

encased
in a floral card box.

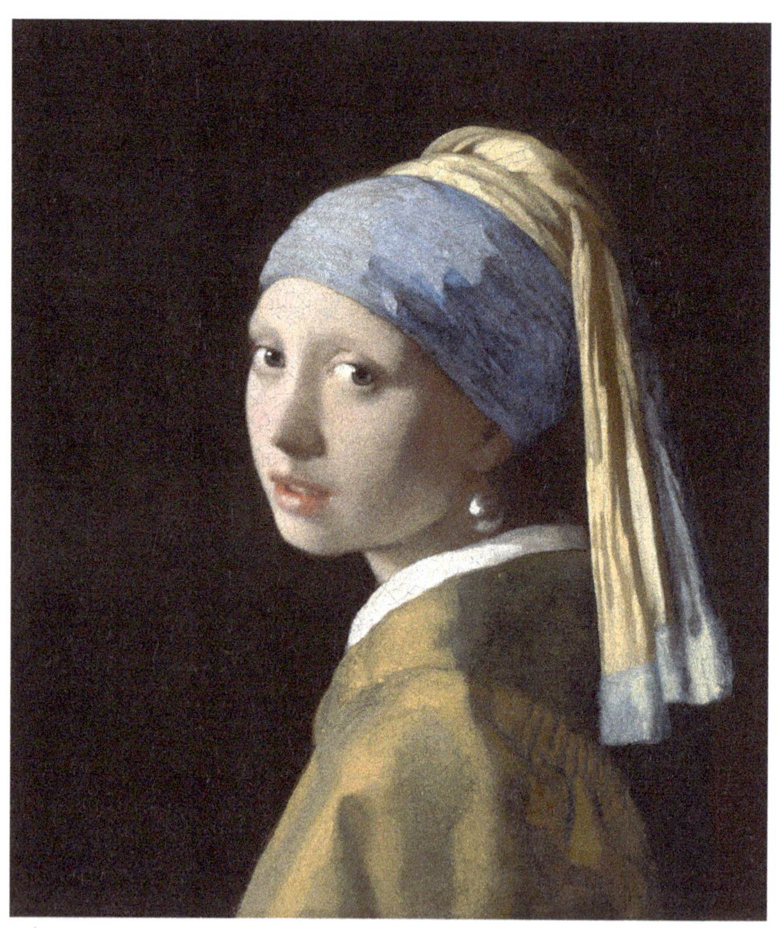

Johannes Vermeer, *The Girl with a Pearl Earring*

YOU HAD BLOOMED LIKE A TULIP IN SPRING

—Johannes Vermeer, *The Girl with a Pearl Earring*, 1665

"I'm now married" was the first thing you said,
my hungry fingers yearning to touch
your luminous skin.

The blue-and-gold scarf on your head,
the golden jacket made you shine
as bright as the sun, our constant chaperone

when we were young. Yet, now a wall of darkness
stood between us. You left, stopped at the threshold
of the room, met my gaze for the very last time,

the liquid pools of your eyes, your soft lips parted,
about to explain what I already knew
from the glistening pearl earrings I had given you.

SOLITUDE

—Edward Hopper, *Automat*, 1927

I

She drinks a hot coffee alone
in a 1920s automat. Outside, a cold winter
evening in New York. She hasn't taken off
her green coat with fur around its collar and cuffs.
She wears one glove, the other hand warmed by
the warm cup that she holds. Two radiators are
not enough to shelter her against the frozen
darkness outside, where the gaping mouth of an
endless tunnel stands ready to swallow her up.
Like a faded flower with drooping petals, the brim
of her hat hides the top half of her face, her eyes,
and covers her ears, her guard against a world of noise.

II

Alone, she has come from work
Her bare neck and legs are stamps
of defiance, her matching hat and dress
proof of a formal occasion. The automat is
her haven, the hot coffee her secret addiction,
the night her time away from the rush
of the Roaring Twenties. Two rows of lights
shine upon her, a splash of red
in front of the window mocks the outside darkness.

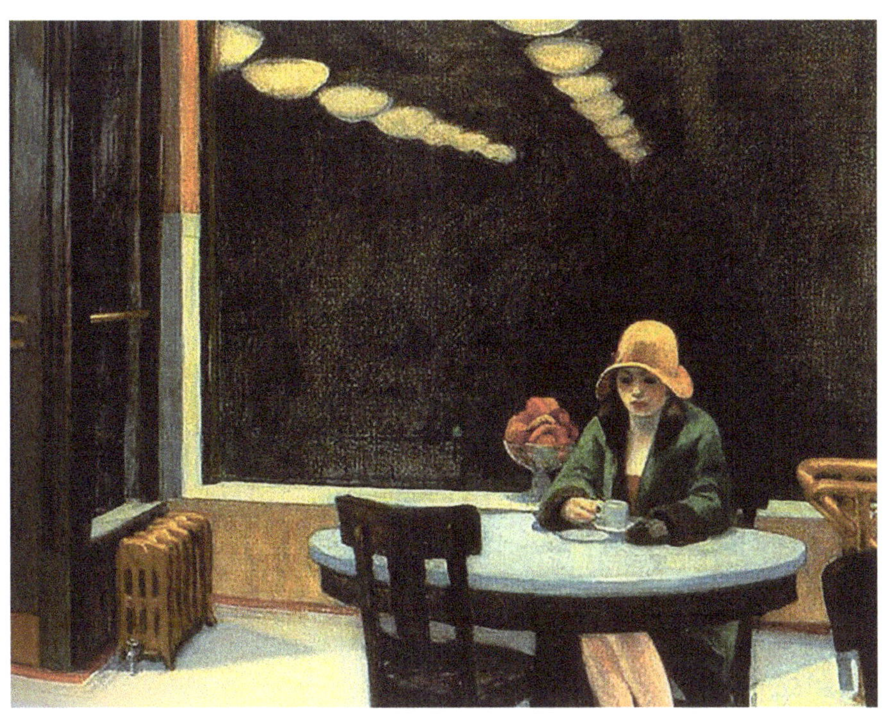

Edward Hopper, *Automat*

THE ART OF KILLING

—Édouard Manet, *Bullfight*, 1865–66

A choreographed dance.

The dancers? Three *matadores*, six
picadores on horseback, nine
banderilleros, one sharp barbed stick
in each hand, and three
mozos de espadas. The music?
The crowd's *Olés*, sung with
a feverish fervor that blinds
more than the sunlight radiating
in the arena, more than the gold
sparkling in each *matador's* suit
of lights. The dancers lure
six bulls to dance, one at a time.

The *matador* baffles the bull by waving
a red *capote*. *Olé!*

A *banderillero* stabs the bull in the shoulders
with two barbed darts. *Olé!*

More of the *torero's* waving dance. *Olé!*

A *picador* follows by piercing
the bull's neck with his lance. *Olé!*

Angered, the bull charges the horse,
knocks it down. More waving,
more barbed darts, *Olé! Olé!*

Weakened, blood oozing down its back,
drool flowing down its neck, the bull stops.
Now is the *matador's* best chance to pierce
its aorta with his steel sword. *Olé! Olé! Olé!*
What an artistic act!

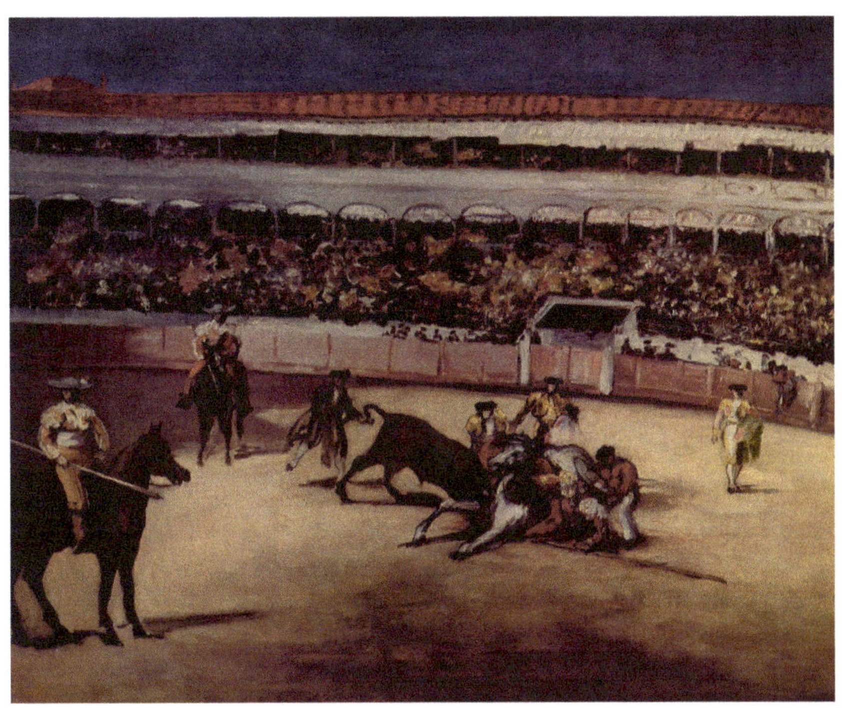

Édouard Manet, *Bullfight*

THE GREY MONOCHROME PALETTE OF WAR

—Pablo Picasso, *Guernica*, 1937

In the room of the Museo Reina Sofia
in Madrid, the mural towers over me, engulfs my
entire field of vision. Twenty-five and one-half

feet long, eleven and one-half feet high, I
am swallowed up, taken inside its guts. I
am in Guernica, Northern Spain. It is April 26,

1937. Under God's eye, Nazi planes drop their bombs
upon a helpless town, while most young men are away on
the front lines of the Spanish Civil War. Death and dying

consume me. A mother clutches
the lifeless body of her child, pain cutting through
her face, her tongue a dagger. A wounded man lies

on the ground, one severed arm still holds a broken sword, his
other hand is mutilated, eyes wide open with the blank
stare of relieving death. A house is on fire, its flames shooting

into the air while engulfing a woman who pleads with the sky
to end the destruction. Another woman rushes out of the crumbling
house, an oil lamp balanced in her extended arm, its small flame strong

enough to shed light upon the darkness, strong enough to guide
the injured woman who is bleeding from the knee across the path
away from the mass of distorted faces in agony, dislocated eyes,

and the dismembered bodies whose parts rot together in a canvas
of chaos. At the center of the scene, a wounded horse screams
in pain, a spear piercing its side. Parts of its body are tattooed

with newsprint ink, reporting a loss that not even a beast like the bull
to the left with its dark body and white head can understand.

NO FREEDOM WITHOUT MARTYRS

—Francisco de Goya y Lucientes, *The Third of May 1808*
(Los Fusilamientos de la Montaña del Príncipe Pío), 1814

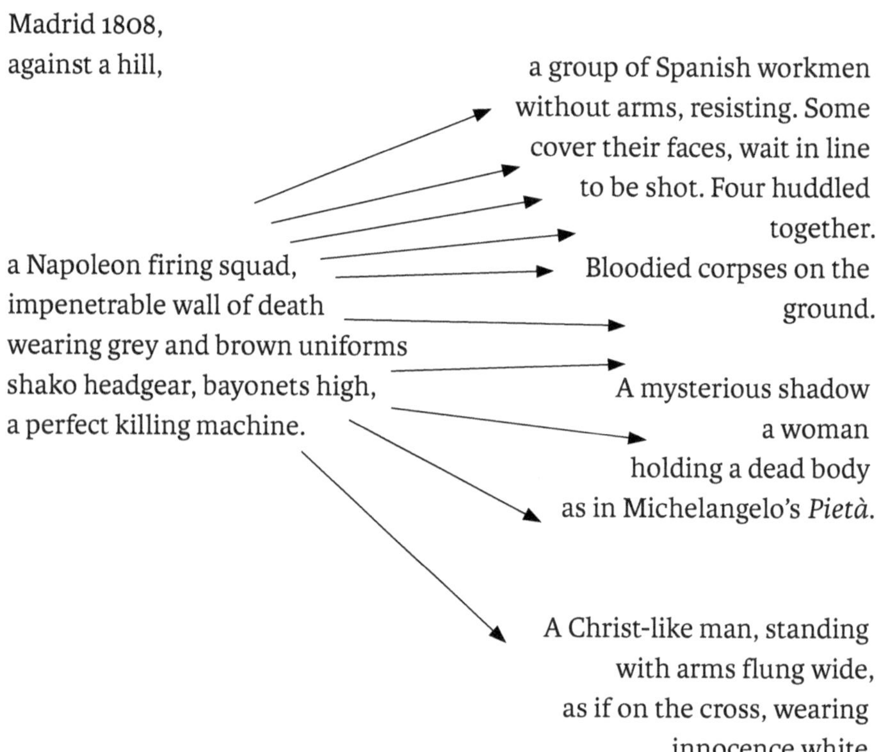

Madrid 1808,
against a hill,

a Napoleon firing squad,
impenetrable wall of death
wearing grey and brown uniforms
shako headgear, bayonets high,
a perfect killing machine.

a group of Spanish workmen
without arms, resisting. Some
cover their faces, wait in line
to be shot. Four huddled
together.
Bloodied corpses on the
ground.

A mysterious shadow
a woman
holding a dead body
as in Michelangelo's *Pietà.*

A Christ-like man, standing
with arms flung wide,
as if on the cross, wearing
innocence white

The Monastery of Doña María de Aragón stands
solemn in the background. The sky
wears black mourning. The stars
have put out their lights.

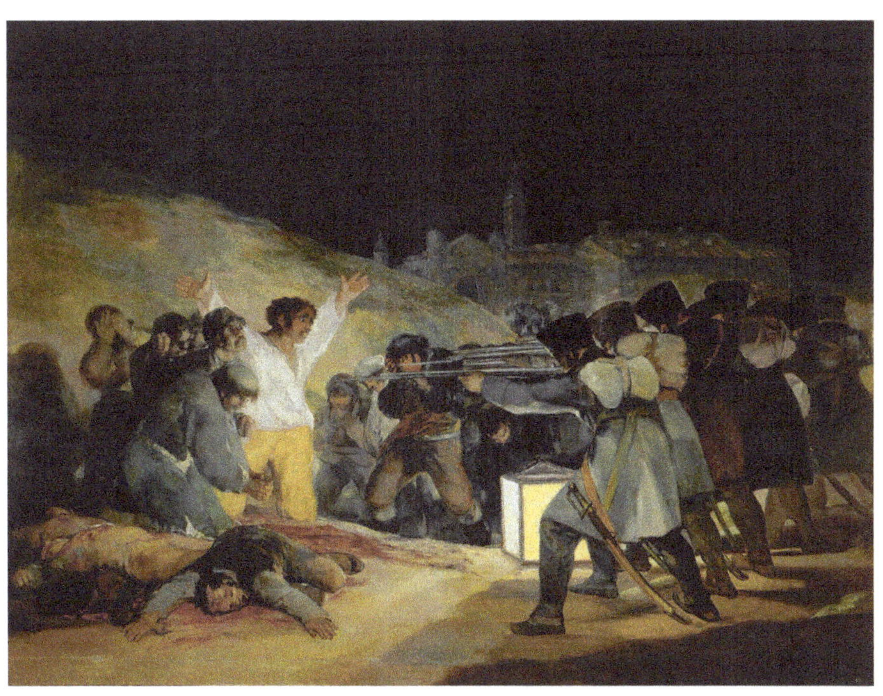

Francisco de Goya y Lucientes, *The Third of May 1808*
(Los Fusilamientos de la Montaña del Príncipe Pío)

IMPERMANENCE

—Jessie Willcox Smith, *I Love My Little Cat,* c. 1930

In the cozy shade under the apple tree
in your grandma's garden, the sweet
breeze prompts the branches to bow
down in your presence, offering
their fruit, red and big like
your heart that now hurts
more than when you
fell and skinned
your knees
in the
past.

Luna stretches after her cat nap and meows her
way to you, her lime green eyes warm like
the grass kissed by the sun in a summer
evening. You pull her close and hug
her, her body relaxing at your soft
but will-not-let-you-fall grasp
while you whisper, *Never*
leave me, Luna. Be
like the moon in
the night
sky.

BETTER TO DIE STILL STANDING THAN TO LIVE KNEELING DOWN

—Octavio Ocampo, *Visions of Quixote,* 1989

I look old and tired, bags under my eyes, untamed hair
in my Van Dyke beard and receding on top of my head,
criss-cross lines on my face and neck, squeaky door
hinges as joints. Indeed, I am old and tired. My years
as a knight-errant winning honor and glory for my love,
Dulcinea del Toboso, have shortened my life.

I filled my past with adventures while riding my noble
steed Rocinante at the side of my loyal squire Sancho
Panza. I fought giants transformed to windmills by Frestón
the enchanter, stopped the funeral of a man believed to be
dead, was beaten senseless defending defenseless women
and children, lived in the Duke's castle, while fending off
the fake sexual advances of fifteen-year-old Altisidora,

I was challenged to duels by other knights, all the while
perceived as an old crazy dog to be mocked. Now that
my time to depart this world has arrived, I am too old
and tired to continue pretending I am a knight who can
restore the chivalry code—bravery, courtesy, honor, and
courtly love. No more am I Don Quijote de la Mancha,
but Alonso Quijano. I could do worse than to die knowing
I tried to free my world of monsters, enchanters, and humbugs
who wished to change me into someone I am not.

VI

THE WOUND IS THE PLACE WHERE THE LIGHT ENTERS YOU

—Rumi

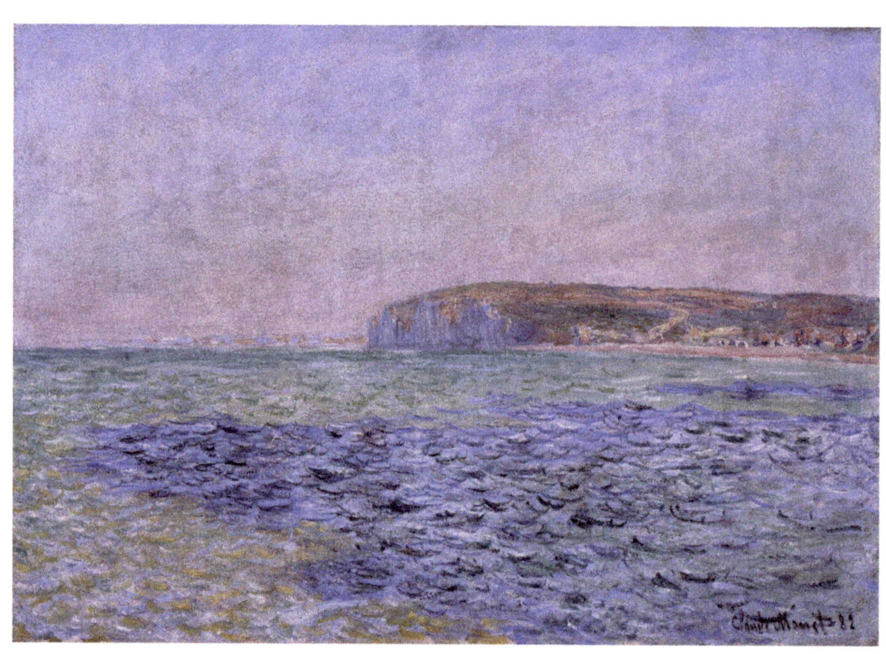

Claude Monet, *Shadows on the Sea at Pourville*

NO LIGHT WITHOUT THE SHADOW

—Claude Monet, *Shadows on the Sea at Pourville,* 1882

"Where there is much light, the shadow is deep"
—Johann Wolfgang von Goethe

One luminous day on the beach at Pourville,
the water glistens like a tranquil mirror, reflecting
the cloudless sky. Some beach-goers daydream
on the shore, listening to the gentle sound
of waves that lap the sand. A big cliff oversees
the palette of colors in the sea, teals, greens,
crisp whites touched by golden brushes coming up
from the golden sand in its most shallow parts.
A darker blue shadow advances
from the east with caution, as if not to scare
the lighter parts, since the brighter the light,
the deeper the travel to uncover its darkest whys.

CONSUMED BY PAIN

—Frida Kahlo, *Pensando en la Muerte (Thinking about Death)*, 1943

These past days I have been thinking of death.
The image of the skull and crossbones has settled
on my forehead between my furrowed eyebrows,
a window I don't want to open.
Yet I stand before the tree of life,
its thick and thorny veins injecting energy
through its dark green leaves.

How much longer can I endure this pain that ties
me to my bed? Its iron-made chains cripple
me like the iron handrail that impaled me
through my pelvis on that bus ride
years ago. How much longer can I endure
a life without living?

Dear Death, cradle this barren body of mine to the grave!

BLOOD-STAINED ESPERANZA

—Frida Kahlo, *The Tree of Hope, Remain Strong*, 1946

I wish I could sit tall on a throne of wood,
feet firm on the ground—no wheels
that slide—dressed in my red *Tehuana* costume,
waving *la bandera* de la Esperanza. I wish

my bones alone could support my back,
and the steel brace I'm forced to wear was made
of pink cloth, a plaything to hold in my lap.
Each time the moon is reborn, I wish

its glowing orb would blind me to the blood-
written words, the blood-soaked tip and tassels
that taint my flag of hope. Yet,
the bursting fire of the sun swells

with the truth: my past is a broken spine,
legs, vertebrae, fractured pelvis and collar
bones, uterus and abdomen punctured
by a handrail when a streetcar crashed

into my bus. Open scars as fresh
as my surgical wounds still bleed as I lay
on a hospital gurney, my back maimed.
Now tears dry on my cheeks, the way the sun
beats down on my earth, a barren desert like my womb.

I am falling through the cracks
of my withered landscape.

VINCENT'S NIGHT SKY

—Vincent van Gogh, *The Starry Night*, 1889

Take me to that place in the night sky
where the winds wrap the stars spiraling
them closer to the crescent moon.

Let me be the morning star, visible
only at dark, before sunrise,
glowing softly in the east.

Make me float over the sleeping town,
nowhere near its dreams and its nightmares;
help me surf the nebulous clouds.

And if you cannot, place me in the highest
branch of a cypress tree, where I can touch
the roiled blue heaven with my fingertips,

higher than the church steeple,
far from the shackles that bind me
to the Saint-Paul asylum.

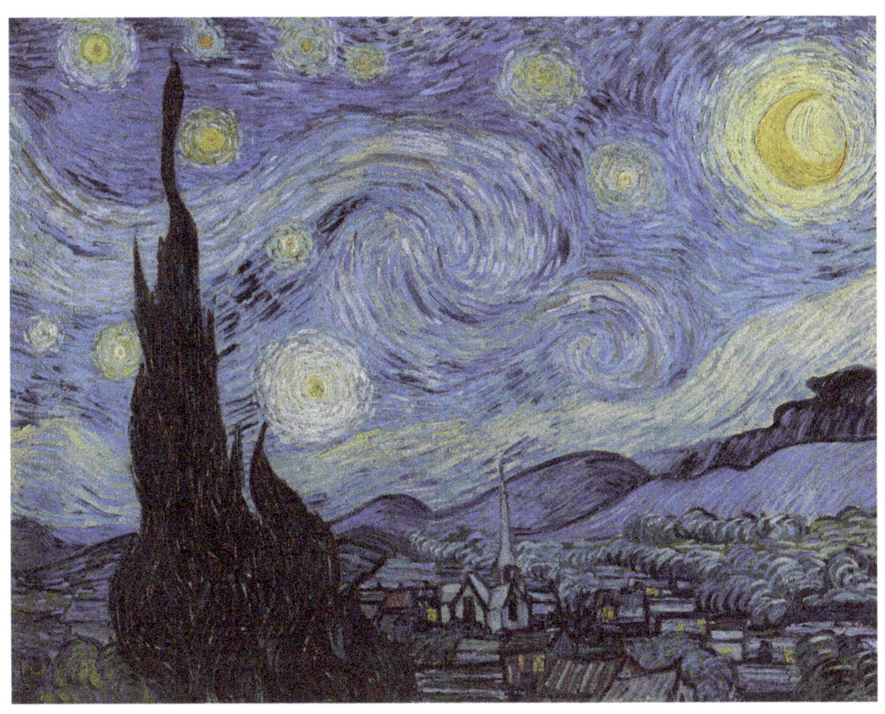

Vincent van Gogh, *The Starry Night*

A ROAD TO THE UNKNOWN

—Vincent van Gogh, *Wheatfield with Crows*, 1890

I stand in the middle of a golden wheatfield,
long stems and leaves moving to the steady rhythm
of the winter winds. The sun has set, the sky wears
its deep blue satin, here darkened by

clouds, there brightened by hidden stars.
Like Moses' Red Sea parted by God, vast fields break
into two, separated by a clear road, a road towards
infinite space, where gravity can't push me down,
where I can't fall; no more wounds, blood, or scars.

A flock of black crows draws near,
their mission to guide me to the end
of that road, the road that saves me
from myself and my afflictions, and yet
a road to the unknown.

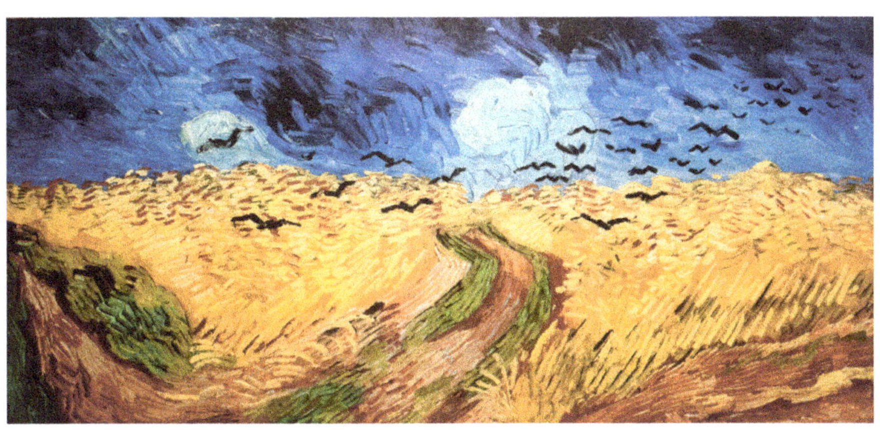

Vincent van Gogh, *Wheatfield with Crows*

THERE PASSES DEATH

—Salvador Dali, *The Horseman of Death*, 1935

the skeleton man, setting off on
his westward march towards the land of the living.

He knows no rush, but never stops, his outstretched arm
an invitation to those who have been chosen to cross

with him the threshold. He'll show the way on
his walking horse, all bones, no flesh, its lush mane

and tail untouched by decay, oblivious to the pain
of a wooden stake thrust though its back leg.

They must pass a thick wall of cypress trees before
a ruined tower, its mourning howls echoing the remnants

of past glories and lost battles,
ports of departure to the unknown, where

birds fly abreast white and black where a rainbow
slices through dark clouds, drowning in a sea

of fire on the other side like a village swallowed
by a fast-moving landslide.

EL DÍA DE LOS MUERTOS

—Octavio Ocampo, *Skull,* 1991

Fresh loaves of *pan de muerto* fill the shelves and big
baskets sit on the floor of my bakery, some decorated with
bones out of dough, others arranged as if skulls. As J.G. Posada
once said, "*todos somos calaveras,*" we will end up without
flesh, only bones. Eggs, flour, yeast, sugar, a dash of anise,
is all that it takes to raise up the dead in the oven.

I've prepared my altar at home: a picture of *abuela* Lupe,
abuelo Joaquín, *tío* Favio, *tía* Marta, without forgetting
my precious dog Ollie, all standing next to flickering
candles and around marigold petals which are scattered
to guide them away from their gravesites each year on
the first two days of November.

I must lay out the *ofrendas*. I will place jars of water to
quench their thirst after their long journeys, loaves of my
best *pan de muerto* to dunk into hot chocolate, *mezcal* and
pulque for the men, *atole, mole negro,* and all kinds of fruit.
I will sit in the middle, wearing my smock on top of my shirt,
the big breadbasket covered in a white cloth upside down on
my head, to look like a *calavera,* and we will dine together.

PABLO'S BLUES

—Pablo Picasso, *The Old Guitarist*, 1903

The lights went out when you shot yourself—
a cold winter evening at a Café in Paris.
When I heard the news, the whole world turned
blue, a dark forest at night—
I'm lost—
the bottom of the ocean—
I'm drowning.
The sky, the roads, the cars,
the buildings, the parks, the shops, the bars,
my studio, my bed, my clothes,
my paintings—all blue . . . like my blue
heart, which cries tears of blue despair.

An eighty-year-old man in a twenty-year-old
body, I wander the streets at night, barefoot,
worn clothes barely covering my bony
body. I fall and drag myself to the curb only to see
myself reflected in an old man, a guitarist, sitting
against a shop window, his legs curled in, his gray
head leaning against his left shoulder as if it was
too heavy and he was too tired to keep it straight, or
maybe, he's trying to hold on to what brings
some light in his blindness—his Spanish
guitar, sighing chords of pain where she's touched
by his frail fingers, strumming a blue life.

CONDEMNED TO LIVE

—Kay Sage, *Le Passage*, 1956

Stripped of your warmth, nothing
covers me but a loincloth loosely
wrapped. In no time,
the winter snow will shrink, then, crack

the soil on which I stand. It will spawn
raised welts on my bare shoulders, though
I am too numb to know. I refuse
to move. Instead, I sit on sharp, angular

rocks that I stack to mark the passage
of time. I look out
at the barren wasteland ahead of me—
I have given my back to life. The sky
is an ocean of muddy waters. It calls
me to the dark place where you lie now.
I wait for it to descend, engulf me. I
will not resist. I've been condemned
to live when I want to die.

THE VISITATION

—Gerald Moira, *The Silent Voice*, 1898

Since her mother departed this world
to join the dwellers of the deep unknown, she sits
nightly on the cold stone ledge by her backyard door.
Three willow oaks stand sentinel, bare arms ill-suited
to offer warmth. She wears the night like a cloak,
the only light scattered stars ceaselessly blinking
to stay awake. She stares into nothingness, her indigo
eyes watery as an icy pond on a clear day. Moon pale,
she brings her hand to her chest, as if trying to hold
the weight of the empty space. She

can't feel her mother's crooked fingers
around her wrist or her thin lips brushing
her cheek, whispering, *I was there when you*
were born and many years after that; you are
strong. Live your life; I've already lived
mine. I'll be here   *when you die.*

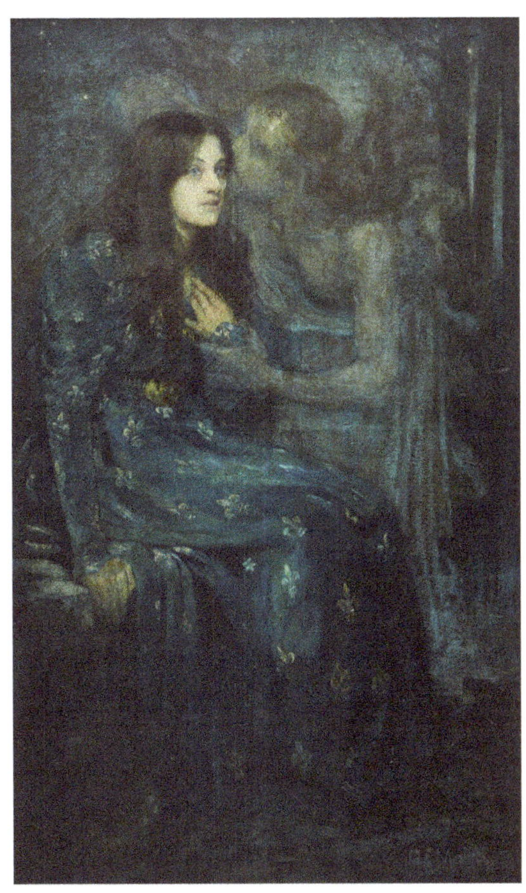

Gerald Moira, *The Silent Voice*

ABOUT THE ART

Images that appear in this book are in the public domain.

[15] Salvador Dali, *Ravel's Bolero (Le Boléro)*, 1946. Oil on canvas. 14.1 x 9.3 inches (36 x 23.8 cm).

[19] Remedios Varo, *The Juggler (The Magician)*, 1956. Oil and inlaid mother of pearl on board. 35.8 x 48 inches (91 x 122 cm). Museum of Modern Art, New York City. www.moma.org

[20] Joan Miró, *The Garden*, 1925.

[22] Gustav Klimt, *The Kiss*, 1907 or 1908. Oil and gold leaf on canvas. 70.8 x 70.8 inches (180 x 180 cm). Österreichische Galerie Belvedere, Vienna, Austria.

[24] James Bullough, *Linger*, 2020. Acrylic and oil on panel. 19.5 x 23.5 inches (50 x 60 cm). jamesbullough.com/painting

[25] Remedios Varo, *Dead Leaves (Les Feuilles Mortes)*, 1956. Oil on cardboard. 29.1 x 23.6 inches (74 x 60 cm).

[26] Michelle Constantine, *Dance of Passion*, 2012.

[31] Adele Kindt, *The Fortune Teller*, 1835. Oil on canvas. 33.6 x 42.5 inches (85.5 x 107.5 cm). Royal Museum of Fine Arts Antwerp, Belgium. www.kmska.be

[32] Kadir Nelson, *Heat Wave*, 2019. Giclee on watercolor paper. 20 x 24 inches (50.8 x 60.9 cm). store.kadirnelson.com

[33] Salvador Dali, *Girl at the Window*, 1925. Oil on cardboard. 41.3 x 29.3 inches (105 x 74.5 cm). Museo Nacional Centro de Arte Reina Sofía, Madrid, Spain. www.museoreinasofia.es

[36] Vincent van Gogh, *The Bedroom*, 1889. Oil on canvas. 22.4 x 29.1 inches (57 x 74 cm). Musée d'Orsay, Paris, France. www.musee-orsay.fr/en

[41] Zdzislaw Beksinski, *Untitled*. www.wikiart.org/en/zdzislaw-beksinski

[42] Doris Clare Zinkeisen, *The Human Laundry: Belsen, April 1945*, 1945. Oil on canvas. 31.6 x 39.3 inches (80.4 x 100 cm). Imperial War Museums, United Kingdom.

[44] Francesco Hayez, *Vengeance is Sworn*, by 1851. Oil on canvas. 93.3 x 70 inches (237 x 178 cm). Liechtenstein Museum of Fine Arts, Vaduz, Liechtenstein. kunstmuseum.li

[46] Leonid Afremov, *Boat by the Lighthouse*.

[51] Rene Magritte, *The Lovers II*, 1928. Oil on canvas. 21.1 x 28.8 inches (54 x 73.4 cm). Museum of Modern Art, New York City. www.moma.org

[52] Remedios Varo, *The Lovers*, 1963. Oil on board laid down on masonite. 29.8 x 12 inches (75.8 x 30.5 cm).

[53] Amrita Sher-Gil, *Sumair*, 1936. Oil on canvas. 22.2 x 36 inches (56.5 x 91.6 cm). National Gallery of Modern Art, New Delhi, India. ngmaindia.gov.in

[54] Edvart Munch, *The Scream*, 1893. Tempera and grease pencil on cardboard. 35.8 x 28.9 inches (91 x 73.5 cm). National Museum of Art, Architecture and Design, Oslo, Norway. www.nasjonalmuseet.no/en

[56] Juan Lucena *¿Qué Haremos sin Ellos? (What Will We Do without Them?)*, 2020. Mixed technique in linen. 150 x 120 inches (381 x 304.8 cm).

[60] Horace Pippin, *Domino Players*, 1943. Oil on fiberboard. 12.7 x 22 inches (32.3 x 55.8 cm). The Phillips Collection, Washington, DC. www.phillipscollection.org

[62] Neena Sethia, *Contradictions of Being*, 2021.

[64] Lilly Martin Spencer, *Peeling Onions*, 1852. Oil on canvas. 35.9 x 29 inches (91.4 x 73.7 cm). The Memorial Art Gallery, Rochester, New York. mag.rochester.edu

[67] Leonardo da Vinci, *Mona Lisa*, 1503-19. Oil on poplar wood. 30.2 x 20.8 inches (76.8 x 53 cm). Louvre Museum, Paris, France. www.louvre.fr/en

[69] Johannes Vermeer, *The Girl with a Pearl Earring*, 1665. Oil on canvas. 17.5 x 15.3 inches (44.5 x 39 cm). Mauritshuis, The Hague, Netherlands. www.mauritshuis.nl/en

[70] Edward Hopper, *Automat*, 1927. Oil on canvas. 28.1 x 35 inches (71.4 x 88.9 cm). Des Moines Art Center, Des Moines, Iowa. desmoinesartcenter.org

[72] Édouard Manet, *Bullfight*, 1865-66. Oil on canvas. 35 x 42.9 inches (89 x 109.2 cm). Musée d'Orsay, Paris, France. www.musee-orsay.fr/en

[74] Pablo Picasso, *Guernica*, 1937. Oil on canvas. 137.5 x 305.7 inches (349.3 x 776.6 cm). Museo Nacional Centro de Arte Reina Sofía, Madrid, Spain. www.museoreinasofia.es/en

[76] Francisco de Goya y Lucientes, *The Third of May 1808 (Los Fusilamientos de la Montaña del Príncipe Pío*, 1814. Oil on canvas. 104.7 x 136 inches (26 x 34 cm). Museo del Prado, Madrid, Spain. www.museodelprado.es/en

[78] Jessie Willcox Smith, *I Love My Little Cat*, c. 1930. Charcoal, gouache, watercolor, and oil on board. 23.2 x 17 inches (59.1 x 43.2 cm).

[79] Octavio Ocampo, *Visions of Quixote*, 1989. www.wikiart.org/en/octavio-ocampo

[83] Claude Monet, *Shadows on the Sea at Pourville,* 1882. Oil on canvas. 22.4 x 31.4 inches (57 x 80 cm). Ny Carlsberg Glyptotek, Copenhagen, Denmark. www.glyptoteket.com

[84] Frida Kahlo, *Pensando en la Muerte (Thinking about Death)*, 1943. Oil on masonite. 20 x 15 inches (50.8 x 38.1 cm). www.fridakahlo.org

[85] Frida Kahlo, *The Tree of Hope, Remain Strong*, 1946. Oil on masonite. 23.5 x 15.9 inches (59.9 x 40.6 cm). www.fridakahlo.org

[86] Vincent van Gogh, *The Starry Night*, 1889. Oil on canvas. 28.7 x 36.2 inches (73 x 92 cm). Museum of Modern Art, New York City. www.moma.org

[88] Vincent van Gogh, *Wheatfield with Crows*, 1890. Oil on canvas. 19.6 x 39.7 inches (50 x 101 cm). Van Gogh Museum, Amsterdam, Netherlands. www.vangoghmuseum.nl/en

[90] Salvador Dali, *The Horseman of Death*, 1935. Oil on canvas. 25.5 x 21.2 inches (65 x 54 cm). Private collection.

[91] Octavio Ocampo, *Skull*, 1991. www.wikiart.org/en/octavio-ocampo

[92] Pablo Picasso, *The Old Guitarist*, 1903. Oil on panel. 48.3 x 32.5 (122.9 x 82.6 cm). Art Institute of Chicago, Chicago, Illinois. www.artic.edu

[93] Kay Sage, *Le Passage*, 1956. Oil on canvas. 35.7 x 28 inches (91 x 71 cm).

[94] Gerald Moira, *The Silent Voice*, 1898.

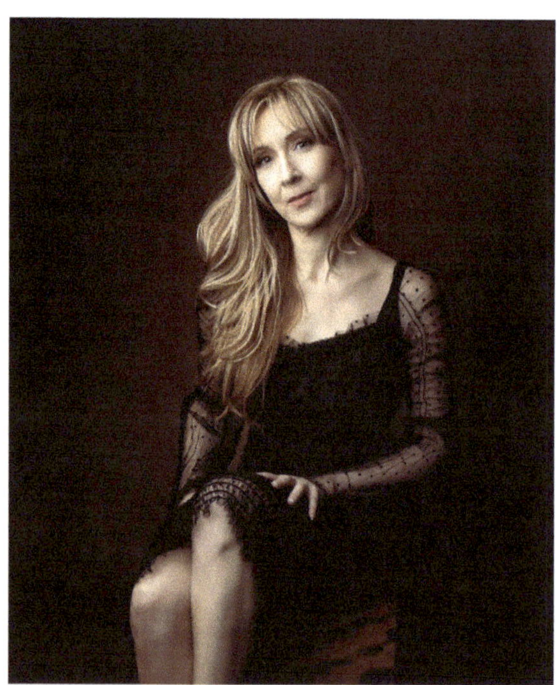

Maribella Portraits, LLC

ABOUT THE AUTHOR

Spanish by birth, **Mari-Carmen Marin** moved to Houston, Texas, in 2003, where she found her second home and teaches English at Lone Star College—Tomball. She turned to poetry at a time when her fears, anxiety, and depressive episodes enveloped her in a veil of dense fog. At first a flicker that helped her take small steps without falling, poetry has become a roaring flame that illuminates her path and warms her through the darkness. Her debut book of poetry, *Swimming, Not Drowning*, was published in 2021 by Legacy Book Press and was the 2022 American Writing Awards Winner for Poetry and Finalist in the Category of Autobiography and Memoir. She also received the Lone Star College Writing Excellence Award in the same year. Since an early age, Marin's dream has been to make a difference in this world, to touch other people's hearts in the way that so many artists have touched hers. She is currently living her dream and will continue living it as long as her duende keeps her company and she has an audience to listen.
—www.maricarmenmarinauthor.com